Leaders Guide
10 Effective Ways to
Get Noticed

Mark A. Miller

Leaders Guide

DEDICATION

My DEDICATION goes to Linda Miller
The Joy Of My Life

Leaders Guide

CONTENTS

Leaders Guide

ACKNOWLEDGMENTS

I would like to ACKNOWLEDGE everyone who I have worked with, whether it be as a leader, people I have led, a peer, family, and friends. The knowledge and teachings that individuals or teams have demonstrated are invaluable to my success. I have never been arrogant as to disregard the idea that everyone I have encountered brings value to me no matter how great or little the impact or significance. I would like to recognize my family and friends that were always there for me, and I was able to extract valuable traits to allow me to be who I am today.

Leaders Guide

1
DON'T HIT THE SNOOZE

Let's face it that no matter how you wake yourself up, whether it be by the alarm of some annoying "BEEP, BEEP", or that one song you absolutely despise comes on to wake you up, it's never a good thing when it happens.

The only thing you want to do is hit the snooze button, go back to sleep, and continue that incredible dream that you were just woken up from.

Why?

Because you are not prepared for the day.

This all stems from a poor routine prior to going to sleep.

Let's change that poor habit into a solid, incredible, positive, and efficient routine, that will change how your day and life will greatly improve so much, you will find that time to do more of the things you enjoy.

That could be time with your family and friends or just time to relax and your job is not taking away from that quality in your life.

Where you need to start is the day before, or even the week before by getting into a routine.

Planning each day to be the same will help with this.

Let's just explore this.

If your routine is to wake up, jump in the shower while you are still half-asleep and hoping that the shower will wake you up but is not effective and you are still sleepy, you pick out your clothing for the day only to find that you have the wrong shoes, belt, accessories or whatever on you and then you are frustrated.

Well now you know that this day is already a day that is going to suck.

So, at this point you are frustrated and going forward you just hop in the car and hope it gets better.

If you're that one-bit quirky person at work, you may be able to pass this off.

I'm going to bet that is not you and how you and not how you meant to show up to work.

Anyhow it's too late and you're going to be late, so you head off to work.

When you arrive, your mind is distracted on how you look and your outfit has you hoping that nobody notices so you will try to hide the way you look, make some excuse, or because you do this a lot, you're worried about being the workplace joke.

Let's eliminate the major stressful miss of your day by doing some simple things with your planning and routine.

Basically, we're going to plan.

Most likely you have a schedule from work each week in advance.

Now you can get each day ready the day before or even your whole week.

Really to do this is not as hard as you might think.

Just be committed to setting the time aside to prepare yourself for your week.

If you do you will save time and frustration daily by knowing you look right, feel right, and your day will be right.

Let me start with a suggestion for those who wear uniforms.

Make sure you have enough of these uniforms, even if you must pay for them yourself.

By doing this the cost of these uniforms will pay for themselves

If for nothing else from lack of frustration in taking your precious time from you.

If you are taking over the counter or prescription medications daily, you will need to get these ready and planned in your daily routine.

Several ways to do this can be done by using a pill minder, a baggie, setting your bottles out on the counter or some way to remind you by getting you into routine of taking these important daily necessities.

If you do these things alone, you will be amazed how much time it will save you from finding bottles in the morning or night now that you have them already out and organized.

Medications are usually a daily routine that doesn't change much so you can get these ready weekly or even monthly.

If you have some kind of daily breakfast and you should have something, you can get that all laid out and ready prior to your time of resting.

Let's say it's just some fresh fruit. There's no reason why you can't get it cut into a bowl and have it ready the night or day before.

Breakfast bar, cereal, coffee, protein drink or anything you want.

Just make sure you have a plan.

Plan on a location on your counter or fridge to have everything ready to go.

Sounds simple right?

It is, but surprisingly it's something people don't even think of.

How much time would that have saved and cleared your mind of frustration and confusion just by being ready and not searching for that thing you forgot, like a clean spoon?

What about the night before? You didn't sleep very well.

Argggggg!!!!

Why didn't you sleep?

Let me guess you did one of these things.

Want to bet that you checked your phone for how many people looked at your social profile, liked your post, checked a text that is not important, talked to your BFF, watched that movie right before or whatever it may be.

These things could be the biggest reason why you can't sleep.

These are life distractions and if you are open to changing these things just a bit, you can end up with improved rest and sleep.

You should practice having a clear mind before you go to sleep.

Really not a whole lot will change in what you like to do except for the last few minutes of the end of the day.

I am sure you have all heard of meditation.

You can make this a personal design and experience.

Set aside the end of the day by eliminating all distractions.

Turn that TV off, radio off, phone off, conversation off, and so on.

Now clear your mind of anything that you are thinking of that will distract you from falling asleep.

It's really kind of easy to do by focusing in on a "happy place" or a soothing nonverbal sound.

Now I am not an expert on this, but it is what helps me and those who I have shared this practice with.

There are several books, videos, and health professionals that can assist you even further and you can explore options that will be most beneficial for you personally.

It is truly suggested that you reach out for professional guidance before you start using sleeping aids, and it should be, in most cases, a temporary solution.

Now you are ready to go to bed and sleep in peace but then that "Damn" alarm goes off in the middle of an incredible dream and you hit the snooze button. Once, twice, or three times.

My suggestion is to move that alarm someplace out of reach.

Why?

You will check the time throughout the night and that will interrupt your sleep and if it is away from you then you can't just hit that button and sleep longer.

The mindset you want is to wake up and greet the day with the best positive intent you can.

Yes, that sounds a bit of Blah Blah Blah, but it is really the truth.

Be thankful that this is a new day and going to be an incredible journey that starts right now.

There is so much to be thankful for that you don't even think of.

Family, friends, money, food, a bed, having clothes, a job, or just being alive now.

Way too often we take the smallest things for granted that someone doesn't even have but would make a difference to their lives.

Think about the surrounding your environment that you wake up in and throughout the areas in your dwelling that will eventually lead you out onto the rest of your journey today with a positive and inspirational outlook.

Use of pictures, quotes, music, or anything that inspires you.

Something that I suggest is that you also change these occasionally so that it doesn't become so common that it's just no longer that daily inspiration.

You can do this by just changing the location if you truly just love them.

These things don't cost you much or maybe they will but remember we want that mindset to change before you even really begin.

Now it's time to clean up.

Yes, that's you.

Just because you have this incredible bathroom and you have the softest towels, best toothbrush, hair care goodies, or just the basic bargain brands you need to clean up.

Now I have lived in both worlds of this and being clean is one of the best ways to be confident.

Do what you can and how you can from top to bottom with your hygiene.

Well, I tired now how about you?

It's time for you to have gone to bed, slept well, cleaned up, taken any needed supplements, had what breakfast you are having, enjoyed your incredible environment, dressed and ready to go, so conquer the start and let's rock this day, week, month, and year.

Your Great Start Leads to an Incredible Finish

Mark A. Miller

For more information on this and other subjects that will benefit you please see my Master Classes and Coaching opportunities at:

WWW.markamillersuccess.com

I Am Committed to Change My:
(List up to 10 but be realistic)

1)

2)

3)

4)

5)

6)

7)

8)

9)

10)

General Notes:

Leaders Guide

2
IT'S NOT JUST A JOB

Crap, I have to go to work.

Are you making this or a similar comment?

Let's face the truth of it, employees will complain about having to go to work.

By the end of this book, you will begin to change that attitude and going forward feel good about it.

So, why are you working.

I would bet it is that you need money.

Guess what, we all need money.

Maybe it because you didn't win the lottery, have an inheritance, are incredibly great looking (but yes you are), want to break from the family and be independent, or maybe you need the insurance but whatever the case might be, you must work.

Other reasons could be that you love to work.

Don't we all?

Just Kidding!

NOT!!!!!

That's being negative but truthfully most people like to keep busy, and work is a great way to connect and feel that you are being a part of something.

So, let's focus on that positive and be that ray of sunshine, okay?

Yes, a bit cheesy, but seriously you need to just be positive.

When you are first starting out and looking for employment you might take any job that hires you at first.

That's okay because as your experience or education grows you start adjusting your likes and dislikes about working.

These likes and dislikes might come from what industry you choose as you are starting out.

Food, retail, medical, construction, or any other areas might look like a good fit at the time, but you might not like it, so it's a good chance you will change.

Could also be the field you choose or the company you work for is limited in growth and you might change employers because you want more from a company.

Your pay or the need for insurance might also factor into where you work.

The focus here is finding a company or field that you will enjoy for now and hopefully for a long time.

You should understand that your employer took the time to advertise, review your application, set time to interview you, hire you and train you.

That's a lot of YOU in there, so yes this is about YOU.

If you think about it, that alone says a lot about the employer's investment in YOU.

Look at it this way, YOU out of a possibility of hundreds were looked at and filtered out.

Then they decided to choose YOU.

Need I say more about YOU and your value that you will provide even before the start of your first day?

Let me share that the cost alone for an employer to even get you to your first day is an incredible investment.

So, as they invested in you and like all investments some kind of return is expected.

When hired be excited and ready on your first day.

Remember the employer wants to know that they chose the right person.

Prior to the start of the first day or on the first day ask questions about the dress code, training, and such.

Just by doing this it will make your first day easier.

It will impress your employer.

Not that your questions might not be incredible insightful, but it will show that you are interested in something about the company and not just there for a paycheck even if you are there for just that.

In many cases you will go through training or orientation so be a good participant.

Be attentive in your training.

Ask questions about anything that you don't understand.

Most companies hopefully have a program that with a new employee they will partner you with a good employee or one that is an effective performer.

This is possibly the first employee you come in long term contact with who might create that everlasting impression on you going forward.

They also may send some negative messages but that might be from personal frustration or have been influenced by other employees.

Mostly, these employees are the ones that you can draw the good out of.

Now as you mix with the staff, you will get employees who are disgruntled.

What to do next is to listen closely to what they are saying.

Pick up some key and common complaints.

Some might complain about something relating to the boss such as they are always watching over or pushing them.

Just know the standard of a company is set for everyone and they are probably an employee who is not performing to the minimum expectations of what the company standards have been set.

Another example might be they are always cutting their hours.

Well, that might be true but why did they hire you?

Most likely to replace someone that is not performing or is not willing to work when needed.

Maybe it's to replace them.

Several reasons for this comment.

The point is that employee(s) or team that you are working with will mostly have something to say about something they don't agree with on policies and expectations.

Again, remember these policies and procedures are in place because without them the company fails.

It's not personal.

Right, wrong, agree or disagree it's there for a reason.

So do what the company expectations are that are in place.

If possible, you may feel you have a better way so make that suggestion.

Many companies have a suggestion box in store or online.

Also asked the why on something for clarification.

Research the company.

You might find some great things about them.

Something that you might want to share with others including your coworkers.

Just remember that you will meet the disgruntled employee of the present or past.

Not always but in most companies.

Put yourself into your work.

Be in the moment and not distracted.

Try to experience the best of work.

Be the example of a good employee.

If you just do your job, you might even enjoy it.

Now if you have tried this field and you don't like it what do you do?

Easy you change!

Too many times someone gets into a field of work, leaves the company, and gets into the same field.

Might be because the money is good, it's easy to do, or something else but if you don't like it, change.

It's never too early or too late to change it.

Remember that the grass is not always greener on the other side if you start over, especially in the same field.

When you talk about your job you should speak positively.

There is something good about most everyplace, and if not, maybe it's you!

Keep that mindset about your job positive and stop listening and sharing the negative feedback that leads to your views being negative and a miserable experience.

One thing is money or pay.

Yes, everyone complains about making more.

If company X is paying more, and you go to them but find you hate it did you make the right choice?

No.

At some point you might want to go back.

Now by some miracle they take you back, you lost credibility.

If that happens be grateful that they did.

As a leader I would not often take someone back because that trust and bond were broken.

Understand that company X is offering more money to these employees so what does that say about company X?

Are they a great company to work for and if so, why are they offering so much more?

If you ask for more money from your current employer expect a NO, but then ask them how you can make more.

Believe me, there are ways.

Most likely they will tell you how by pointing out performance increase raise for being that perfect employee or other career paths.

As you can see, just by having a better outlook that you could enjoy your job more.

It really comes from you and not the employer.

You control that happiness.

Avoid the negative.

Research the positives of the company.

Partner with good employees.

Be happy you are being paid to improve your life and situation.

Change Your Attitude Change Your Day

Mark A. Miller

For more information on this and other subjects that will benefit you please see my Master Classes and Coaching opportunities at:

WWW.markamillersuccess.com

I Am Committed to Change My:
(List up to 10 but be realistic)

1)

2)

3)

4)

5)

6)

7)

8)

9)

10)

General Notes:

Leaders Guide

3
FEEDBACK WELCOME

"I don't want to know."

Yes, you do and here is why.

When you are in a role of leadership or any position with the company that provides feedback mostly everyone really sucks at giving quality feedback.

What I mean by quality feedback is good, bad or in between feedback.

Most employers and leaders are awesome at giving one type of feedback and that's bad or negative.

Why? Because they are focused on things a computer or printout gives to them as a guide of performance.

So, the focus is always on what you are doing wrong and not what you're doing right.

That's because they don't take the time to know more about you and your needs as an employee.

Could be because they are looking for the problem on a page and not the actual barrier.

Now even if the feedback is good, bad, or indifferent there is always a but in there somewhere.

But you could do better on something, and I am sure if you got a but, you feel your efforts are not being recognized, defeated and that BUTT stinks.

So, let's turn that but around and you might have to be the one who gives the feedback on better information your leadership needs.

What?

You tell me to give feedback?

Yes you.

Ask for it or comment back but be specific on how you do it.

Let's explore how to ask for feedback.

You might know when you are having time with the boss by having a specific time set aside daily, weekly, monthly, or yearly.

You must take this important step in the feedback.

Be prepared for it and have it in writing in what response you are prepared to address or feedback you are looking for.

If you are in a leadership role you probably already know some of the feedback, you are going to get from your leadership.

Most meetings with your higher-ups have a time frame set aside for any "other" business or any other questions during your meeting time.

If this is not offered ask if you can have a few minutes to talk about some things that.

In most cases the opportunity can be made but you need to be ready to use them wisely.

When the opportunity comes up point out how you are effectively helping the goals of the company.

This could be you personally or your team you are with or leading.

If it's your team, point that out.

Also include that you help to lead the team to these results.

Basically, you need to credit your team if needed but also include yourself in that credit.

When these conversations come up also make sure you are focused on mostly what the company goals are and how you lead your team in helping with these goals.

You can add some other points in your conversation that might be about the company goals or interest but make these simple conversations.

They might care about the other sharing of information but let's be honest it is mostly show of interest and they like that.

It's the company they think about because it's the company that pays the check.

Without the company they don't get paid either.

Not that it's bad, but it is the truth.

If in giving feedback you have an outstanding employee who you might want to show off, then you should do it.

Doing this shows you care about your employees, and they appreciate it.

Your boss will be able to know who might be next in line for the promotions just by giving feedback.

Other ways of giving feedback are when you get or ask for feedback even if it might be negative or indifferent, be receptive to it.

Ask your boss how you can improve in these areas.

You will be surprised by just that doing, the connection you will have with those above you will change as more positive going forward.

Believe it or not they would rather you do great at your job because they end up with better results on their vison of what they need.

They can point out who, what and why or even teach you better ways.

Good bosses love to show why they might be in their position.

You might even respect them more because they know why you are not performing as needed and they might want to help.

Also, with feedback on poor or average performance show you want to improve and that you care about your performance.

Don't be shocked if in your next discussion you have with your boss that they just might take more of an interest in your performance or career.

Plus, I bet you get a more sincere and welcoming greeting.

So, when these feedback sessions take place, be thankful for them and don't take it personally as to the negative feedback.

Use this information to improve yourself or at least improve your performance.

You don't want to work for years being miserable so take ownership of your feedback time and improve you.

You can always take the positive feedback moments and offer your talents to the boss to help those who could use your insight.

That only makes your job easier and enjoyable.

Thank You

For

Helping Me

Mark A. Miller

For more information on this and other subjects that will benefit you please see my Master Classes and Coaching opportunities at:

WWW.markamillersuccess.com

I Am Committed to Change My:
(List up to 10 but be realistic)

1)

2)

3)

4)

5)

6)

7)

8)

9)

10)

General Notes:

Leaders Guide

4
THE FUN MANAGER

"Party Time!"

This might sound like a great way to be that "Fun" manager and in some ways, it is, but how to balance being the fun leader with the effective leader.

Being just the fun manager will be a major mistake.

Sure, everyone has a manager they like to work with.

The leader who when you see that you are going to work with and know from past experiences it's going to be a great workday.

You might even comment to others or higher-ups that I really like working with this person because they are fun to work with.

Is that you?

Well let's hope so but for the right reasons.

Employees will like most managers that allow them to get away with performing below expectations.

These are the leaders that look the other way with those who want to get away with bad behavior or act up.

They might allow employees to extend their breaks and lunches.

Could be that the leader ignores completion of tasks or productivity, and it creates a poor habit and bad work ethics.

Basically, allow the employees to lead the leader.

So, if that is you and the next day your boss comes in and asks why something wasn't done again and again and you know why, how do you respond?

Well, I was busy doing blah blah blah or employee X wasn't feeling good or slow at their job.

Guess what?

They have heard all that before and in most cases can check if that is all true.

They are not stupid and that's why they are in their position and addressing your performance.

Maybe you had to do all the work because of being the fun manager who would rather be liked than to set the expectations and accountability with your team.

Is that the case with you?

Be honest.

In most situations it's because you want to be liked or fit in with those you work with.

Here is a reality check.

If you are incapable of leading you should consider stepping down, quitting, or best of all changing.

You can do it!

Remember you were chosen to be in this position so do it the right way.

They are counting on you to do what you are paid to do.

Ask yourself, do you want to lose your job because you were the fun manager?

Of course not.

Remember that these employees who consider you the fun manager are not going to pay your bills, quit when you are fired, or in fact care tomorrow.

They are going to look at how they can get away with things from your replacement.

You become the excuse why they didn't perform and the reason why they are still employed.

Let's point out that I'm not saying you can't be fun.

What I am saying is to be who the company wants you to be and that's to be the leader.

Your team or employees, and this includes the great one at times will find a reason not to do something.

Other reasons could be just that one of the employees is having a bad day.

That happens but not every day.

Don't allow that to happen if it's a constant.

Be the leader.

No reason why you can't include when you are working together some conversations about them.

Make some fun conversation by getting to know them a bit better.

People love to talk about themselves.

Maybe bring in treats that are different than the usual treats.

Something unique.

Most of all you need to "win" the team by praising them.

You can praise them individually, in a team meeting or to a higher up.

Look for the smallest of things that others may not notice.

In most cases everyone has something good to recognize.

Not always but in most cases.

If by doing these simple things, you will become the respected manager and maybe even the fun manager.

The team will like working with you.

Remember that you were chosen for your position, and you are the one being paid that rate of pay for a position of importance.

Now step it up.

You'll eliminate that personal frustration, build your self-worth, and just maybe enjoy your job for once like you did before the promotion.

If you don't change you will be starting a new job always with the same problem and that problem, is you.

Being Fun

And

#1

Mark A. Miller

For more information on this and other subjects that will benefit you please see my Master Classes and Coaching opportunities at:

WWW.markamillersuccess.com

I Am Committed to Change My:
(List up to 10 but be realistic)

1)

2)

3)

4)

5)

6)

7)

8)

9)

10)

Leaders Guide

General Notes:

Leaders Guide

5
DOING MORE-NOT LESS

When you are hired by any employer, and you start working on your first day, what is your attitude towards your actual job and duties?

Do you start by already having that mindset that you will not do more than expected or even what they just simply ask of you?

Could be?

When you arrive do you say to yourself, "Man, I just want this day to be over with already", right when you start or just a little into your shift?

If so, then why did you go to work at all?

Why do you even have a job if this is your mindset even before you start or just started?

No doubt this is your mindset in life as well.

So, to be honest is this you?

Then you are that bad employee, filled with excuses and your work ethics need to be addressed.

Let's look at it from the employer's point of view.

They hired you and are paying you so do the job and do it right.

Is that too much to ask for?

Guess what?

NO!

Get that you are entitled and have a everyone gets a trophy mentality out of your head and change it.

Sometimes wanting to do more takes a bit of investigation work.

What is more and how do I do it?

Let's say your employer is asking you to do X, Y, and Z.

If you do X, Y, and Z every day, guess what?

You did your job.

Nothing special.

Just your job.

Let's look at the more.

If you did X, Y, and Z you have extra time then what do you do?

Well, then ask yourself do I really need to slow down next time, or do you seek out that extra work?

Think about when you're in school and the teacher gave you an assignment.

You did it right?

So, if you were like most of us you found the extra time that it gave you as play time and wasted it.

Right?

Not talking about that perfect student but the rest of us.

Remember that most teachers offered extra credit.

Think about that, it's extra credit.

If you were a midgrade student, then how much could you have improved that grade by just doing extra credit.

How much easier would maintaining that average grade been.

If you did that in school imagine how your mindset would be about doing extra now.

Your mindset would have developed that extra work ethic that is missing now.

Your teachers would have excused the poor or missed assignment.

Your family, friends, peers would have looked at you as a hard-working wanting to get ahead person and you might have made that difference of inspiration to someone from that point through their life.

Maybe your grades would have improved, and you got into a great college.

Just imagine that.

Now, we got off track with the education part but if you are a student or parent reading this, then it might help in the early development of a work ethic in the future.

Back on track as we explore more.

Employers invested time and money in hiring you.

You don't think of this, but it costs a lot of money to hire and train you.

You should respect that and be grateful for this opportunity.

What more is can be anything you can do extra after you did X, Y, and Z.

The best way to know what more is would be to ask your leadership or supervisor.

Let me point out that if X, Y, and Z are done and is done right the first time without having to be redone you're done.

When you approach the supervision or leadership make sure you let them know that you have become proficient in what is currently being asked of you and you would like more responsibility.

Maybe not that way but you want to point out that the job you are assigned has been proven to no longer be a challenge for you.

You become that valued employee that would like to help the team and company by doing more.

When you do this expect the look of surprise on the face of the supervision or leadership.

Why do you ask?

Because this is something that is rare and missing in today's work force.

Today people do less and expect more and that's the truth.

Employees complain about working too hard in most companies when they truly are not even doing what is expected or what they are getting paid to do.

Be that difference and example by being the one who does more and wants more from themself.

It doesn't have to be a lot more but something extra to get you noticed.

If you do this enough, you will become the next promotion.

That higher raise.

If you mess up and it's not a major violation, then they don't let you go.

When layoffs happen, you are the one they keep.

Be honest with yourself if you truly want to do this.

If you do you will be surprised as to the difference it makes in your pride and self-confidence.

Again, when layoffs happen, and raises don't it is because you didn't do more and someone else did so they stayed and got a raise or promoted.

Promotions and higher raises are often determined by those who perform best.

It's not that hard and you can change your mindset now whatever stage you are at your work.

Even if you have worked someplace for some time, you can change that average view of you to be an example.

Now let's be the best you know you can be.

Know More

Do More

Be More

Mark A. Miller

For more information on this and other subjects that will benefit you please see my Master Classes and Coaching opportunities at:

WWW.markamillersuccess.com

I Am Committed to Change My:
(List up to 10 but be realistic)

1)

2)

3)

4)

5)

6)

7)

8)

9)

10)

General Notes:

Leaders Guide

6
SPEAKING UP

One of the hardest things anyone can do is to speak with absolute confidence.

Yes, I mean in most cases this is true.

Let's look at the confidence part of it.

Guess what?

Most speakers at most levels are not 100% comfortable speaking in group settings whether it's the first time or they have done it 100 times before.

There is always some bit of uncertainty about the message they are trying to get out.

Believe it or not but it could be that they are somewhat in doubt of the subject matter, how they sound especially through a microphone, how they look, how the messages being received, or could be a million different reasons but as you can see, they get through it.

You are amazed at the fantastic job that they did and how they made it look so effortless.

Let me tell you that at some point they were just like you are now.

So how do they prepare themselves?

They practice what they are saying and doing.

They practice the message, steps, movements, eye contact, and so on.

It is very rarely 100% not planned in some way.

If you are going to be asking a question or providing a speech, you must be ready.

When you are in a group setting with others who may be mostly your peers then this could be a very difficult situation for you.

Why?

Well, you don't want to look like the one who doesn't know the answer to the question or subject.

Right?

You might feel that you are asking or commenting on something and thinking you are the only one who feels this way or doesn't understand.

Let me assure you in most situations you are not the only one with this question or comment, but you are the only one to have the courage and speak up.

After you become the Lion that is hidden inside, you will be amazed as to the new connections you make with others that you have become that Hero.

Yes, a Hero.

Now there is always that person or people who know it all.

They will look at you that way they do or pass judgement to make you feel that you are "less than" who you are.

Just do it anyhow because you didn't like them anyway nor did the rest of your group so just don't care.

It is really that simple.

This is about YOU and not them.

Feeling comfortable now?

Just kidding.

I know you're not!

You should always come prepared with a list of well-thought-out questions when it is possible.

Bring a notepad with well thought out possible questions or comments already on it.

During the session write new or after though questions or comments that might be relative to the setting.

Eliminate any comments or questions that are not important on your prelist.

It is important to pay attention so when your opportunity comes up you don't waste it.

When you are in smaller groups or even one on ones do the same with being prepared.

If you are sitting or stand hiding behind others to hide yourself you are not fooling anyone, so then you become that nobody.

Are you a nobody?

When you become that nobody then you become that nobody by name and you are invisible to the situation and the people around you.

Think about that.

You are being a NOBODY and that's not who you are.

Also don't stress about how you phrase your comment or question.

You want to be clear but it's not important to phrase it perfectly.

One well known quote is "The only dumb question is one that is never asked."

That's it in a nutshell.

Yes, it can be scary but the more you do it the more you get comfortable in not just social situations but in life situations.

Look at it this way if you know the answer you shouldn't have asked the question.

If you don't and others do know the answer, then there is a gap in how the information failed to get to you properly.

A Lions roar can be heard up to 5 miles away so be the Lion.

I Will

Roar

Today

Mark A. Miller

For more information on this and other subjects that will benefit you please see my Master Classes and Coaching opportunities at:

WWW.markamillersuccess.com

I Am Committed to Change My:
(List up to 10 but be realistic)

1)

2)

3)

4)

5)

6)

7)

8)

9)

10)

General Notes:

Leaders Guide

7
DIFFICULT BOSS OR EMPLOYEE

Not everyone has that hard to work with a boss or employee but in most cases, you have one or many of them.

First let's focus on the employee.

It's best to know why you find the employee difficult.

It could be performance or personality.

Maybe you don't like their appearance.

Whatever the case may be.

Look at it objectively at first before you find that they are not a good fit for you to work with or your company.

Some employers have guidelines on how to relate or deal with difficult employees.

Policies and procedures.

Understand that these policies or guidelines are in place to protect you.

Now make sure that you are the one who forms your opinion on them.

Don't let the influence of others form that opinion for you.

One incredible way is that you engage with that employee every chance you get.

Get to know the employee by name.

Provide a simple hello or how are you doing is great to start and means more by adding in their name into the conversation.

The employee might be shy or not sociable, so break the ice!

Another way is to ask a simple how are you doing today.

Focus on today?

If by not knowing them and their situation they may be under a lot of stress, and they open to you.

When you focus on the today you might be able to get to see some pattern such as every Monday, they are difficult.

Might be that something is happening to them weekly.

If it's just an everyday thing, then it could be just them!

Ask about how do they like working here.

This can bring out a flood of information.

The answers might be you find out that they don't make enough to support something or maybe they have another job or the hours they are scheduled are hard to work.

Could be that they are having a problem with another employee.

Whatever they say it might give you some insight into the problem as to why they are difficult.

Maybe they offer information that you can help them with.

Might find that it is difficult for an employee to become a loyal one, at least to you.

Should it be something you can't personally help them with maybe offer advice as to who can help if possible.

For a situation that is just impossible for you to help just show compassion.

Sometimes that is all they need.

Now to be real in some situations it might be that this employee creates problems or blames others so know that is just simply something you can't control.

Try to be the light of the day, if possible, by being positive.

Yes, by being the sunshine daily can be a drag, but you might be the only thing good in their day so try to share a positive.

You will feel better when you are able to help others.

Also, there are those people that no matter what you do refuse to change or improve themselves and it's always someone else's fault.

Without being cruel just be honest.

Don't fill them with empty promises on how they or you can fix the issues or by placing blame on others or the company.

Try these things and if nothing improves, then the truth is it's just that difficult employee.

Now how about that boss.

So, let's be honest, most bosses are difficult in some way.

If you break down the bosses, you have had and if you truly say you like them in every way you are extremely lucky!

Here is how you deal with the boss.

The boss has a bit of arrogance about them or if they don't, they should.

After all they are the boss!

Responsible for a lot and in a position for a reason.

Find the weakness or find the common ground.

Start by asking questions about what they like.

Could be sports, games, movies, books, outdoors or any number of things.

When you find out those things take a bit of interest in them.

Not that you must be the expert in the subject matter but just have a working knowledge of it.

Know you don't have to get into long conversations with them about it, but it will create a comfort zone.

You might not even care about those things but that's what they are doing with you in asking about you.

Hard truth is that it is just conversation to them.

Do the same and find that opportunity for creating a comfort zone.

It might be difficult to find a common conversation ground because people often put up a wall.

They don't want you to know them.

You can ask questions about your company.

Know that a knowledgeable boss will tell you something about everything they know and love to do it.

In fact, it will open the floodgates of stuff you might care less about but let them talk.

They like to look smart even if you know the answer already.

When the opportunity comes up that they don't know something and you do know it, that's an opportunity you don't want to miss.

This will be a great advantage for you.

You can become the SME or Subject Matter Expert by being humble without rubbing it in that you know something they don't.

Show them that you want to share or avoid the subject entirely to not making them feel uncomfortable.

Be welcoming to the boss every time you see them.

Even if it was a bad meeting THANK the boss for the opportunity to learn and improve.

Don't make excuses.

Take ownership of yourself and the team.

After all it is your responsibility.

The point is to find common ground and interest even if it's not real.

Effectively Change Difficult People

Mark A. Miller

For more information on this and other subjects that will benefit you please see my Master Classes and Coaching opportunities at:

WWW.markamillersuccess.com

I Am Committed to Change My:
(List up to 10 but be realistic)

1)

2)

3)

4)

5)

6)

7)

8)

9)

10)

General Notes:

Leaders Guide

8
GO TO PERSON

Hello genius, the incredible you that has all the answers, right?

Well, you may or may not have the answers, but you are the one they are coming to, and you are frustrated because of it.

So, let's solve that issue.

First, you need to know that yes you have all the answers, or you know how to get them.

It could be that you have all the answers in your head, on paper, in files, have the resources or whatever but it is all up to you to give the answers.

Let's explore you being the SME or Subject Matter Expert and you sharing that information.

Let's say employee X comes to you about something they want or need.

They are coming to you and that alone is a huge compliment.

Could be something important or not but that doesn't matter because they need information.

Now did you just grunt, point, or dismiss them?

Better not have because if you know the answer or not you shouldn't give that employee the impression that you don't care.

At that point they tell everyone that you're an idiot or the truth is, you just don't care.

Is that the kind of place you want to work at?

No, it's not and neither do they.

Now just think about being labeled the company idiot.

Yep, you are the idiot now.

So, if you know the answer why you don't you take the time to show, teach, or direct that employee.

Guess what?

In just one moment you become a person of knowledge and trust.

This is where employee Z comes to you and then you take the time to show, teach, and direct them.

Now you become the hero.

Get it?

Idiot to hero.

Well now employee X comes to you because Z spread the word how incredible you are with being the go-to person.

Once again you show, teach, and direct them with full understanding of what needs they might have.

Suddenly you are spending all your time answering questions or solving problems as you are the "go-to" person on everything.

Now A through W starts to come up to you about anything and everything.

Great that they feel that trust and confidence in you but now you can't get your work done because you are always busy with other problems or creating solutions.

So, what do you do?

In case you didn't notice I left out Y.

Y is the first one you spent time with on everything so Y can help you stop becoming the only go-to person.

In fact, you spent so much time with Y that they know more than you and have the answers to most everything.

See by sharing all that knowledge with Y you have freed up your time and now instead of you they go to Y.

So, you and Y share that responsibility but mostly Y is handling it.

Well, that's a lot of letters still coming to Y and occasionally to you which is still filling up your day and you are struggling with getting your work done.

A thought occurs to you that what if Y leaves for a promotion or another job and it all falls back to you.

Just remember that you are the HERO and not the IDIOT.

You and Y took the time to educate X and Z by showing, teaching, and educating them.

Now it's X, Y and Z helping A through W with everything and anything so that they all become the SME (Subject Matter Expert).

So now genius your team basically has become self-sufficient.

Just remember that all this started with you.

Now you will only handle the new questions or concerns that the others can't answer.

You complete your work and are far less stressed.

Get it?

The point is you don't need to be the only one with all the answers.

Allow your team to be helpful because in many cases it brings them a sense of pride.

The team really doesn't even bother you, except when they needed help or guidance on something they are not getting answers to.

When you do this, you build teamwork.

You become the one they still come to when they are stuck.

The one they trust and respect.

The Hero not idiot.

Then your alphabet team will share that it all started with you, and you should be proud of that.

I Am
The
Solution

Mark A. Miller

For more information on this and other subjects that will benefit you please see my Master Classes and Coaching opportunities at:

WWW.markamillersuccess.com

I Am Committed to Change My:
(List up to 10 but be realistic)

1)

2)

3)

4)

5)

6)

7)

8)

9)

10)

General Notes:

Leaders Guide

9
WHEN TO BE THE HARD-ASS

Let's face it, the world today is full of fluff and there is a new way of leading.

No matter if it's right or wrong it is still the way you must lead in most businesses.

There will come a time when you need to be that hard leader.

So how do you become comfortable in doing this?

Really, it's not as hard as you think.

Let me say that going forward, this is not meant to offend anyone, but you need to know how it is going to be.

Remember that being hard, harsh, or direct is not always a bad thing.

If fact it is a part of being a leader.

First be prepared and patient as you begin the process of being hard, direct and at times harsh.

Make sure you have a full understanding as to what issues you will need to address or correct.

Now you need to find out if this person was provided with a full understanding of what you need to discuss with them.

If not, you might need to step back a bit and start from the beginning as to what the employee understands.

Now what I mean by understanding is does or did this employee get the same information as everyone else in the same or similar way that is sufficient for them to know that there might be a problem?

If they did then the answer is yes, they did have the right information.

If you have any doubt, then start there.

When you need to go forward you might be the unpopular manager and address the issue or situation.

You at this point must be sure you follow whatever your company policy is.

Most. if not all companies have an ER or HR department to consult and guide you.

I would highly encourage you to consult with them first.

Now after doing that you are ready to proceed.

Let's be clear that this is for all employees.

In most situations it is a bit hard to discipline a good employee.

This employee might be 99.9% gold but this time they messed up.

Don't look the other way at what the issue or violation was that needs to be addressed.

If you do and make this a habit of turning the other way you will have to do with for everyone, all the time and that's just a nightmare going forward.

Plus, that's not fair.

It's so important to be fair and consistent in all situations.

By being fair across the board then your integrity will never be questioned.

If you don't address even the smallest issue or situation you must not address, it for all your employees and that's not what the pay you to do.

You are the leader.

Let's look at the ones that deserve it or bad employees first.

This is not as easy as you think.

These are the employees who will challenge you on everything you are about to discuss.

They are smarter than you might think because they are already prepared on their issues because they know how to avoid it being their fault by passing blame on to others.

When these discussions take place, it is extremely important to keep calm from the start to the finish.

They are looking to frustrate you and play on your anger.

You must speak directly about the subjects or issues at hand.

Do not stray from focused conversation.

Again, this is a way the employee will get you distracted from what the issues are, and the focus off them.

Slow down when you speak and be loud enough, so they hear you.

Set a time limit on your conversation and make sure the employee knows that there is a time limit.

During the conversation if it seems that it is going to take longer than planned interject and remind the employee that this conversation needs to move forward.

Stretching conversations is also a way that employees will use to avoid all the issues that need to be discussed.

When closing give them the opportunity to provide feedback.

You might need to let them know at the beginning of the conversation that this time and the limit of time will be provided so you can avoid some extended side points they might want to bring up.

When you allow the feedback, you can have it either verbal or written but stay focused on the issue not all the distracted information that they will bring up.

Before they leave review the issues, concerns, and outcomes again but make it brief.

When your time limit is done you must THANK them for their time.

Yes, THANK them even if you're angry or frustrated.

After they are gone write down any comments you would like to make or personal wins or improvements for the next time you need to do this.

It's not a bad idea to get feedback from anyone you had as a witness.

For the great 99.9% gold employee guess what.

You do the same.

This is not Rocket Science but remember you must be fair and consistent.

The difference is in most cases, but not all, you will breeze through the good employee.

They might give you a hard time because they don't understand why you are doing this to them.

Tell them it's because you must be fair and consistent with all employees on subject matters or violations.

They will understand.

A few things to keep in mind.

Use your prior notes or experiences as a reference as to what went right or wrong.

You're doing everyone including yourself a favor by being this leader.

You are helping them correct something.

Could be that it's improving their performance on something, or you could be leading them to a different career path.

Remember that It's not a bad thing and don't take it personal because it's your job.

You are the leader.

It's Not Easy Being the Boss, but it is Necessary.

Mark A. Miller

For more information on this and other subjects that will benefit you please see my Master Classes and Coaching opportunities at:

WWW.markamillersuccess.com

I Am Committed to Change My:
(List up to 10 but be realistic)

1)

2)

3)

4)

5)

6)

7)

8)

9)

10)

General Notes:

Leaders Guide

10
IT'S YOUR REVIEW

Woo Hoo! It's performance review time and I'm going to rock this."

Or that's what you say to yourself.

So, after an hour you emerge from the review and say "Dang, that really sucked."

"I thought I did what was expected of me and I am just an average employee?"

How many times in a review have you had this happen?

Well, if your supervision or leadership is truly fair and honest as well as if you have been truly honest with yourself this should not be a shock to you.

In fact, you should have known the outcome.

Let's review the process to know what to expect and it is simple to do.

What is expected of you is the question, and often never asked.

Why?

Because you don't want to do more.

Let's face it, you are most likely there to do the job or less if you are not asking for what the expectations or extra is.

If you show up on time daily, do the work that is expected and effectively, you generally have a good attitude, and don't complain.

Guess what?

That's an average review and nothing more.

That's what you get paid to do and that's what you did.

If you expected better, you didn't do extra so here it is average.

The full-time employee works an average of 1800 hours a year minus time off and holidays, so it is a lot of time working.

In that 1800 plus hours what extra did you do?

Did you do extra work daily or cover a shift or hours a couple times?

Is that extra enough?

The short answer is no.

Yes, you did help a couple times but that's not really going above and beyond.

If you did this a lot then in some area or category if the reviews are broken up that way, you might get a better review in that category or area.

It's also a reminder that you got paid to do that extra shift and I bet you really needed the money so that's why you said yes and not because you cared.

Now I don't want to discount that because you might do it a lot and be the one who is always willing to work extra shifts so again yes you might need to be recognized for that.

How about your attitude at work.

Do you grumble?

Only do what's expected?

Slow start to your working shift?

Kill time?

Just basically a bad attitude?

Guess what?

It's not even average.

Employers will kind of look away at average employees that complain occasionally but truthfully you should be ranked below average.

Basically, you are not doing your job as a team player when you are this employee.

You're creating a lack of production with others by doing because you have lowered the morale of the team.

You become that employee everyone does not want to work with.

Let's explore that outstanding hard and efficient worker but is always late or has callouts.

Well guess what?

You have the below average rating as well.

You are expected to show up on time for work.

Yes, I'm sure you have 1 million excuses.

The truth is, you plan poorly, and you base your work ability to bail you out.

Let's explore the other side.

Maybe you're the one that always shows up on time.

Works hard, efficient and is always looking for more or helps others or the company.

The one that is that cheerleader at work and fills in when and where needed.

Now you come up with an average review.

HELL NO!

We don't want that to happen.

Know your value before your review and be prepared.

Employers often forget how valuable you are.

It's not that they might not care but really it can't be overlooked that you are a value and it's because you are not the problem.

Let's remind them of this and be prepared.

Keep a journal on yourself.

Write down the "extra" value you provide daily.

This becomes work on your part, but do you want that promotion or raise or not?

Make a habit of your journal daily or weekly.

It's not that hard if it becomes a habit.

Set up a one on one with your supervisor or leadership weekly or monthly and review what your value is or what extra you have done even if it's on your own time.

When review day comes have these notes ready.

Organize them by category if you can so if reviews are divided by personal, team or company values you can point those things out.

Give a copy of your notes to your supervisor or leadership long before your review so they can make any adjustments that they may have forgotten to include in preparing your review.

Basically, you need to sell yourself.

The plus on this is your review will go smooth.

You will get the correct review, raise, position and so on.

The recognition you deserve needs to be pointed out on what's the extra value you provide.

Now the average or below average employee needs to also do this Journal as well.

The reason is when your review is done you will already know why you are not getting a raise or very little of one.

One common feeling from employees is that the "Bust their ass" but look at your ass is it broken?

Many of the poor reviews come from lack of understanding of expectations or just plain overvaluing your worth verses being honest of your value.

Don't Question Your Value

Mark A. Miller

For more information on this and other subjects that will benefit you please see my Master Classes and Coaching opportunities at:

WWW.markamillersuccess.com

I Am Committed to Change My:

(List up to 10 but be realistic)

1)

2)

3)

4)

5)

6)

7)

8)

9)

10)

General Notes:

Leaders Guide

Leaders Guide

This is a general and basic guide to some key leadership qualities while improving your ability to stand out and be noticed.

This is a journey only you can decide to take.

When you commit to taking steps to improve yourself then only you can decide to grow or stay the same.

Yes, it is difficult when you are improving yourself when people tell you that you are changing.

Understand that you are not changing the you that you are but the you that you are pretending to be.

If others can't support your decisions on change, then you should evaluate who is your support group and who is not.

Don't allow the negative people in your life to alter the greatness hiding inside you.

Allow me to help you with this journey.

www.markamillersuccess.com

Leaders Guide